GOD'S FORGO

M000196696

By JOHANNES HOOGERBRUGGE

God's Forgotten Pillars

Author: Johannes Hoogerbrugge

© Copyright: Johannes Hoogerbrugge, 2019

ISBN: 978-1-945423-15-4

All rights reserved by Author
PUBLISHED BY:
Five Stones Publishing
A DIVISION OF:
The International Localization Network
randy2905@gmail.com
ILNcenter.com

Endorsements

I found this book challenging, confronting and inspiring as the needs of the most neglected segment of the contemporary church were practically presented by a man who has dedicated his life to caring for the aged. In the rush to reach the next generation we must not neglect the last generation. Reaching the next generation represents our Godly ambition; reaching the last generation represents our Godly responsibility.

Michael P. Cavanaugh
President, Elim Bible Institute and College
Lima, NY

In his short but meaningful book, God's Forgotten Pillars, John Hoogerbrugge does an excellent job of providing both a vision and a blueprint for ministry to the aged. Even better, John encourages churches to avail themselves to this vital opportunity by incorporating the church body without overburdening pastoral staff. If your church has a vision for ministry beyond itself, this book will help!

Bob Santos
President, Search for Me Ministries
Indiana, PA

John Hoogerbrugge has written this important book based on a lifetime of caring ministry and first-hand experience. As I read God's Forgotten Pillars, I was struck with Rev. Hoogerbrugge's sensitivity, insights, and care of our seniors who are often forgotten. Understanding older adults and what they face is documented with care as well as practical recommendations by those who are invited to make visits and contacts to family members, friends, and church members.

This is a book that is practical and is faith-filled. I encourage people of faith, pastors and laity, to be challenged by the content and committed to touching the forgotten pillars who often live alone or are in institutions of care. Rev. Hoogerbrugge understands the need to remember and care for older adults. I have known him and have seen his ministry in daily life in the Lutheran Centers of the synod I shared as bishop. I encourage you to read this book and share it with others in the Christian community where you live. It will make a difference in your care for our elderly.

Bishop Donald J McCoid
Bishop Emeritus, Southwestern Pennsylvania Synod
Interim Bishop, Metropolitan New York Synod
Evangelical Lutheran Church in America

For busy pastors, the task of caring for God's "oldest friends" can easily be ignored or minimized by the demands of other pressing parish priorities. With touching stories, John Hoogerbrugge has illustrated the various needs and challenges of frail older church members, and his practical examples and techniques for addressing their spiritual needs are very relevant. In particular, he stresses the importance of maintaining good membership record systems that don't allow home-bound members to fall between the cracks and be forgotten, and he encourages the use of trained lay visitors to supplement the congregational pastoral care with older members. This book is timely and a "must read" for anyone working with older church members.

The Rev. David C. Baker, Ph.D., Director
Regional Interfaith Chaplaincy Services
Middletown, Maryland

God's Forgotten Pillars is a must read for every pastor, lay leader, and family member who desire to give the appropriate care to elderly citizens among us. Johannes Hoogerbrugge's experience, wisdom, and research as a pastor, chaplain and son provides practical insight to help the reader remember, reward, and bring the needed release to those have often given so much.

Rev. Chris Ball, President
Elim Fellowship
Lima, NY

Chock full of theological, pastoral, and clinical wisdom, this highly accessible book from a wise pastor and chaplain should be required reading for all church leaders, as well as for all who have family members who are no longer able to care for themselves. Biblically rooted, practically sound, pastorally gentle, and broadly ecumenical, it offers both an incisive critique of the church's current elder care practices and invaluable counsel on how to correct them. John Hoogerbrugge has learned much of great value over many years of ministering to and with elderly saints, and we are all much richer for him endowing us with this treasure box of insights that challenges us to tend better those saints among us who are aged and infirm. It is a grace-filled invitation to embrace more faithfully the biblical command to honor our fathers and mothers well. They deserve our best, and we will be truly blessed for offering it to them.

Rev. Dr. Sheldon W. Sorge,
General Minister of Pittsburgh Presbytery
(Presbyterian Church USA)
Pittsburgh, PA

"God's Forgotten Pillars" is an honest wake-up call not only for pastors but for our entire culture. It calls us to rethink the way we treat those who have seemingly "aged out" not only of our communities of faith but of our society as a whole. The touching stories and wonderful words of guidance provided within the pages of this book are a must read for all who those deal with older adults and the on-the-job knowledge is especially important for seminarians, pastors, church boards, and long-term caregivers. As a pastor and an aging adult, I am not only touched by the wisdom found within these pages but am grateful for them and pray that those who care for me learn from this insightful and important book.

Rev. M. Susie Esseck, Retired
Evangelical Lutheran Church of America

In my four decades of full-time pastoral ministry, John Hoogerbrugge remains the most dedicated pastor to the Senior population that I have ever encountered. In his book, "God's Forgotten Pillars", John shares his incredible depth of knowledge and experience in a way that is insightful, instructive and inspiring. He provides us with a virtual 'handbook' for the most sensitive and sometimes difficult encounters that those who are called to provide support and care for our seniors will ever face. Every believer will need this information at some point, and most everyone of us who want to honor and bless 'God's Forgotten Pillars' will benefit from reading and using it for future reference.

Pr. Jay Passavant, Founding Pastor
North Way Christian Community
Wexford, PA

Acknowledgledgments

The following people have been a great inspiration to me over the years and have supported me in the writing of this book. My thanks to each of them.

My wife, Dawn, who has encouraged, supported, and partnered with me in forty-five years of marriage and ministry.

The Rev. Dr. David C. Baker who was my mentor during the first six years of my ministry as a long-term health care chaplain.

Rev. Wilfred Goetze who was my colleague and fellow chaplain for the twenty years I worked at both health care facilities.

Mrs. Lynn Fletcher, friend and artist who designed the cover for this book.

All those who helped with the editing of the book for their valuable input.

All the people who have contributed stories for this book. It was their stories that motivated me to bring awareness to this need in the Body of Christ.

Table of Contents

Preface

In 1980, when I was still a young pastor, I accepted a call to a small country church which did not keep an official membership roll. Anyone who attended on a regular basis was automatically considered a member. I had been there about two and a half years before someone informed me about an elderly couple who used to attend but had become shut-in. When I went to visit them for the first time, the pain of being ignored by the church was obvious. Apparently, the previous pastor had not provided them with very much pastoral care. Even though I visited them several times over the next few years, I felt like I was never fully accepted as their pastor. When one of them passed away, the surviving spouse asked a long-time friend of theirs, who was an out-of-state pastor, to come and do the funeral. I still continued to make contact with the surviving spouse until the Lord moved us away from the area a few years later.

After we left that church, we spent a couple of years preparing to go overseas as missionaries. After living overseas for seven years, we returned to the United States and I took on secular employment. During those seven years the surviving spouse also passed away and I completely forgot about this couple.

Then in 1997, I was offered a position as one of three chaplains for two long-term care facilities; a position I held for twenty years until my retirement. Because of that experience, I have developed a very different understanding of pastoral care to the older adults among us. I thought a lot about this couple in my position as a chaplain and had I understood the needs of the older adult back then, my ministry to this couple would have been very different.

I have discovered that many of the older adults among us, who were once pillars in their churches, have become God's

Forgotten Pillars; not forgotten by God, but forgotten by the church. The number of the residents at the two long-term care facilities where I ministered who told me that no one from their church visited them was much higher than I first realized. I also discovered that many churches automatically dropped someone from their rolls if that person had not attended and/or sent them money for a year. And, more often than not, no one from the church had contacted them to see why they no longer attended or to see if they needed help from the church. In a very real sense, these Forgotten Pillars who had become shut-in could be classified as lost sheep. Again, not lost by God, but lost by the church. Yet, Jesus told us to leave the ninety-nine and go after that one lost sheep (Luke 15:3-6).

The purpose of this book is to enlighten the church to the spiritual needs of the older adults and to offer suggestions as to how the church can effectively minister to them. It is birthed through my own experience of working with older adults for twenty years. I believe it was the late Gerhard Frost, a former professor at Lutheran Northwestern Seminary, St. Paul, Minnesota, who once said that we can identify with young people because we were young once, but we don't understand the needs of older adults because we haven't been old yet.[1] It is hoped that this book will give the reader a better understanding of what it is to grow old and how the spiritual needs of older adults are different than that of younger adults.

The names of the people mentioned in the stories in this book have been changed to protect their privacy; but all the stories are true.

Chapter 1:

Why Older Adults Are Being Forgotten

I remember that as a youngster, we were always taught to respect our elders, address them as Mr. or Mrs., listen to them, and learn from them.

After I graduated from high school, I got a job working in a company that employed many men from our church. I was suddenly thrust into a situation where many adults whom I had always addressed as Mr. at our church were now addressed by their first names at work. It was difficult for me to change the way I addressed them but eventually I found myself addressing them by their first names at work and addressing them as Mr. at church.

Cultural View of Older Adults

Around this same time, late 1960s and early 1970s, many teenagers began to address their parents by their first names instead of Mom or Dad. Their parents wanted to be thought of as friends, not as authority figures. Although this was not intended to show disrespect for older adults, I wonder sometimes if this might have partially influenced the way we look at older adults today. There is no denying the fact that there has been a cultural shift in how we respect and treat the elderly. This shift is not only found in our western culture, but also in our churches.

One of the other cultural shifts has been the emphasis on youth and staying young, which affects how we view ourselves and our children, as well as older adults. Many of us do not want to admit that we are growing older so society is always coming up with new ways to keep us looking young—physical exercise, make-up, beauty creams, cosmetic surgery, Botox treatments, hair coloration, etc. We don't want to look old; we don't want to look our true age. Instead, we want to look young and have people think that we are younger than we really are.

In part, this is because we no longer see as being beautiful older adults who have wrinkles, sagging skin, thinning hair, and cellulitis. And we don't want to end up looking like them. We want to retain our youthful looks. This is also one reason why older adults are becoming more isolated—we don't want to visit them because they remind us of what we will become as we grow older. An unintended result is that older adults become isolated and lonely. Keith G. Meador and Shaun C. Henson write, "How far we have come in our modern culture from growing old as a sign of wisdom, long life as a symbol of God's blessing, gray hair as a crown of glory, and the dutiful care of those who are no longer able to care for themselves. In a church dictated to by a therapeutic culture, we trade these in largely for a premium on youth and surface beauty, rather than acknowledge our aging as a gift from God within the inevitable temporal contingencies of this age."[1]

Our emphasis on trying to remain looking and feeling young makes it more difficult for older adults to accept their frailties and makes younger adults look down upon those who have become frail. I am at a stage in my life where I am learning that I can't do as much as I once could. I have to admit that I am getting older and am becoming more dependent upon others to do some things that I had no difficulty doing when I was younger. I also have to admit that I occasionally get impatient with those who are older and who take longer in doing things. But the older I get, the more I realize that some day that will be me.

Carole Baily Stoneking writes, "By the late nineteenth century ... an image of the second half of life as literally barren of possibilities gives birth to modernity's attempts to 'master' old age rather than yield to it, to eliminate rather than explore the final stage of life."[2]

Stanley Hauerwas and Laura Yordy add, "In our society the single most striking portrayal of old people is their loneliness. Friendship with the elderly is almost unimaginable, as our very conception of what it means to be old is one of isolation. This isolation compounds with frailty, lack of usefulness to the world, dislocation from home and possessions, forced dependency, and nostalgia to construct a pitiable picture of a person who is unloved, and, in many ways, unlovable."[3]

Old age cannot be "mastered" or eliminated. Instead, we need to accept it and respect it for what it is. In doing so, we will give honor where honor is due rather than relegate our elderly to a life of isolation and loneliness.

Coupled with our desire to remain looking and feeling young is our emphasis on usefulness and productivity. Older adults who are no longer able to be productive feel useless and unneeded. Unfortunately, society and the church have given in to this notion and no longer seek out the older adult for wisdom or for assistance for things that they can still do. This not only makes the older adult feel useless and unneeded; it also makes them feel unwanted. This happened to my mother-in-law. She continued to live alone for a number of years after she was widowed. However, her own health was gradually failing and eventually she moved in with two of her children alternating between them. But while she was still living on her own, her pastor made a very hurtful comment. Although he did not intend it as such, it still hurt her. Her church was having a spring-cleaning day in which everyone was asked to come and help spruce up the church after a harsh winter. But her pastor told her she didn't have to come if she didn't want to. He didn't want her to feel obligated to come and help because he thought it might be too much of a hardship for her. Unfortunately, my mother-in-law erroneously interpreted this statement to mean that he did not want her there, that she was not welcome. This greatly upset and discouraged her. It would have been far better if her pastor had encouraged her to come and assist with things she could do sitting down, or just to come for the socialization.

Along with the decrease in physical and sometimes mental abilities, we also associate old age with a decrease in intelligence and wisdom. Aging has become viewed as unacceptable and, therefore, we develop prejudices against older adults and no longer accept the wisdom which they still possess. The result is that we stop consulting them for advice and suggestions. Yet if we take the time to sit and converse with them, we will discover a wealth of knowledge, wisdom, and understanding. I learned so much from listening to the retired pastors who were residents at the care facilities where I worked. We need to remember that people of all ages are valuable not because of their productivity or usefulness, but because they are created in the image and likeness of God.

Along with society's declining interest in the older adult, there is an increased interest in our youth. More and more programs are being established for children and teenagers while fewer programs are found for older adults. This is noticeable in the cutbacks of government programing and assistance for them. Unfortunately, the church has followed suit. In an attempt to keep the youth interested in the church, many churches have greatly increased their funding for youth programs including the building of gymnasiums and hiring youth pastors. Yet few churches hire pastors to minister to the elderly.

While I believe that the church needs to emphasize ministry to our youth, it must not come at the expense of those who for decades have given of their time, talents, and finances to make the church what it is today. We need to see a shift in the church's attitude toward older adults and realize that they have more to offer us than what we may think and we need to show them our appreciation for their past contributions to the church. As Stoneking writes, "This biblical ideal of adulthood affirms that all ages of life are equal in God's eyes."[4]

Biblical View of Older Adults

One of the best ways for the church to shift its attitude is to look at how scripture treats the elderly.

A look at the Old Testament reveals that early humankind lived hundreds of fruitful years before they died. Seldom is there any reference to uselessness or unproductivity of anyone who was old, and when there is, they are still treated with respect.

Noah was 500 years old when his sons Shem, Ham, and Japheth were born (Genesis 5:32) and he was 600 years old when he entered the ark which he had just finished building (Genesis 7:6-7).

Although Abraham did not live as long as Noah, he was 100 years old when he and Sarah had a son Isaac (Genesis 21:4). In fact, Paul commends Abraham's faith stating, *"He did not weaken in faith when he considered his own body, which was as good as dead (since he was about a hundred years old), or when he considered the barrenness of Sarah's womb."* (Romans 4:19).

We also have examples in the New Testament starting with Zechariah and Elizabeth who in their old age gave birth to John the Baptist (Luke 1). Then there were Simeon and Anna who in their old age prophesied over the baby Jesus in the temple (Luke 2:25-38). From all accounts it appears as if the apostles Peter, John, and Paul continued to serve God as leaders in the church well into old age.

We need to remember the words of Job in Job 12:12, *"Wisdom is with the aged, and understanding in length of days."*

The Ten Commandments tell us to honor our parents, yet the Pharisees re-wrote them when they said, *"Whatever you would have gained from me is Corban (that is, given to God)"* (Mark 7:9-13). Jesus had harsh words for them because *"in the name of God"* they were no longer honoring their parents. Paul also condemns those who did not provide for their families saying, *"He has denied the faith and is worse than an unbeliever."* (1 Timothy 5:8).

Richard and Judith Hays write, "Equally important, perhaps, are the things not said about older characters in the New Testament. Nowhere in the biblical canon are they pitied, patronized, or treated with condescension. Nowhere is growing old itself described as a problem. Nowhere are elders described as pitiable, irrelevant, or behind the curve, as inactive or unproductive. Nowhere are they, as in so many Western dramas and narratives, lampooned as comic figures. On the contrary, they are seen as the bearers of wisdom by virtue of their age."[5]

I realize that all pastors are extremely busy in their ministry and they have to devote their time in a multitude of directions, but churches need to find a way to include older adults, not exclude them. Besides, it is not the sole responsibility of the pastor; it is the responsibility of the entire church.

I grew up in a church which took seriously its call to minister to everyone in the congregation. Our congregation was split up into geographical districts, one for each elder. Every autumn, the elders formed teams of two and each team visited every family in their districts so that every family in the church was visited. This was on top of regular visits that the pastor made to shut-ins throughout the year. The elders of my childhood church took their responsibilities seriously and assisted the pastor in ministering to the church family. As a child, I did not look forward to those visits, but looking back on them now I see their benefit because they showed everyone, including the shut-ins, that they were important.

In the following chapters and in the Addendum, I will give some practical suggestions as to how we can effectively minister to the older adults in our congregations. However, at the same time, we need to realize that pastors cannot be the only ones who need to do this. It takes the whole church to make the older adults feel welcomed and appreciated. It is my sincere hope that this book will help equip the church to minister to older adults in their congregations, especially to those who are shut-in.

Chapter 2:

The Unique Needs of Older Adults

Are the needs of the older adult any different than the needs of others? While in many respects they are not, in some ways they are. Each age group has similar needs to other age groups, yet each also has unique needs specific to that age group.

Some of the greatest needs for older adults are socialization and a sense of belonging and worth.

Importance of Visitation

We have already mentioned isolation and loneliness. Many older adults lack sufficient socialization for various reasons. One reason is that many of their friends are confined to their homes or long-term care facilities, or have passed away, so they have fewer friends with which to socialize. Another reason is that they may have had to give up driving. This not only limits their ability to go and visit others, but also limits their ability to go shopping, to church, or other activities they used to attend. Even though they may still be able to socialize over the phone, a phone conversation is not as beneficial as a face-to-face visit, and many older people have difficulty hearing on a phone. Many older adults also have children who work or have had to relocate for their work, so they are not available to visit very often. When older adults become confined to their homes or long-term care facilities, they may also feel imprisoned. Many of the residents at the two long-term care facilities where I worked have told me that they felt like they were in prison because they rarely left the building; and if they were confined to a locked dementia unit, they felt even more imprisoned.

As their own ability to function decreases, they not only feel useless and unneeded, they also become more dependent upon others. This makes them feel that they have become a burden to their families and friends. They experience a role-reversal with which many older adults struggle because it requires them to redefine their roles. Instead of parenting their children, their children begin to parent them. They also give up their roles as elders in their church, or as business and community leaders. Their wisdom, knowledge, expertise, and understanding are no longer sought out by others which may lead to a feeling of rejection. Whereas they used to give to others, they have become recipients from others. Instead of being givers, they are now receivers. This can easily lead to discouragement and even depression. In fact, many older adults in long-term nursing care facilities experience symptoms of depression and receive anti-depressants.

One way we can help them overcome these feelings is to enable them to find purpose and meaning to their lives. Regular visitation reassures them that they are still valued, appreciated, and needed which helps them to find purpose and meaning. It validates them for who they are, not for what they do, especially if they aren't able to do very much anymore. Our society places tremendous emphasis on doing and not enough emphasis on being, which is contrary to God's Word. When we look at the gospels, Jesus spent time with the people; he was more concerned with who the people were than on what the people did. God calls us to be more than he calls us to do. When we spend time with shut-ins, we affirm and validate them for who they are.

It is sometimes difficult to convince the older adult that declining health, becoming shut-in or bedfast, no longer feeling productive, etc., does not mean that God has removed His presence or His love. It is even more difficult to convince them of this when the church neglects them. When we visit and spend time with shut-ins, we affirm that God has not forgotten them.

Paul says in 2 Corinthians 5:20 that we are Christ's ambassadors; we represent Him here on earth. God reveals Himself to others through us. When we neglect our shut-ins, we deprive God of the opportunity to reveal Himself to them in their time of need, so they begin to feel that God also neglects them.

Joel James Shuman reminds us that as a church, we have a duty to care for our brothers and sisters in Christ. He states, "The church is a baptismally reconstituted, extended family whose members affirm a fundamental obligation to care for one another in a way that can certainly be described as familial."[1] Just as we would normally care for our physical next-of-kin, we also need to care for our spiritual family.

Experiencing Neglect

Joanne, a resident at one of the long-term care facilities where I used to work wrote this, "I made sure that they had my new address, phone number, and e-mail to keep in touch. Now here it is, eight and one-half months later, and I have not received one phone call or visit from anyone in the church. Where are those people in the church who I thought were my friends, prayer warriors, and support? Have they forgotten me? ... I do not understand. I have been a member of [my church] for over fifteen years attending church every Sunday either sitting in the front pew for each service or participating by singing in the choir. I was active in Women's Bible Studies, belonged to a weekly home group, served in the church's outreach ministry in the community, was a faithful tither, prayer warrior, etc. etc. Where is this church family that I was a part of for all those years? Do they really care about me? I feel alone, abandoned, disappointed, and even a bit angry; so angry that during this difficult time in the life of our family, I haven't even contacted them for prayer support because I feel they don't care. Is the only thing they are concerned about my tithe which I continue to send every month? I don't want to have these thoughts, but how can I think otherwise when there has been no contact?"

Joanne had been a very active pillar in her church, yet her church had forgotten her. The hurt is evident in this note she gave me.

Lisa showed me a letter she had received from her church. The letter said that because she had not attended her church nor contributed financially for over a year she was being dropped from her church's roll. She had received this letter in the mail, so they had her address and they knew where she lived. I asked her if anyone from the church had come to visit her, phone her, or inquired about her health. They had not. Instead, she received a very cold letter stating she was being dropped as a member from a church which she had attended most of her adult life.

John, a man in his mid-fifties with Downs Syndrome, came to us after a fifty-one day stay in a local hospital. Because he lived in a group home and it would take three hours to get ready for church, he had not been active in his church for quite some time. Unfortunately, no one from his church visited him while he was in the hospital nor at the group home where he lived. When I called the church to inform them that he was now in one of our nursing homes, I was informed that the church's new pastor did not know him and would not be coming to visit him.

Isolation, loneliness, neglect, rejection, and abandonment are very real for many older adults. Regular visitation helps to overcome these feelings. In Hebrews 13:5, God says, *"I will never leave you nor forsake you."* Romans 8:39b says that nothing *"will be able to separate us from the love of God in Christ Jesus our Lord."* These are God's promises to us, but if we are not God's ambassadors and do not visit our elderly shut-ins, these promises become empty words. In fact, it was one of our residents who used the phrase "empty words" in a conversation with me because she felt God's promises were unfulfilled in her life.

Older adults experience all kinds of losses besides the deaths of loved ones and friends. They also experience the loss of independence, functionality, self-care, etc. Being abandoned by their church adds to those losses, and also adds to their feeling that God's promises in the Bible are just empty words. When that happens, they sometimes begin to question other things about God. Does God still love them? Is God punishing them for their sins? Are they good enough to go to heaven? What other suffering is God going to put them through before they die? Why is God doing this to them when they so faithfully served the church and helped those in need? Is their faith still strong enough? These are very real questions which I have been asked many times. And if the church neglects them, these questions could easily plague them for the rest of their lives. They need answers to these questions; answers that only the church can provide. (See chapter Six on ministering to those who are grieving loss.)

Susan Pendleton Jones and L. Gregory Jones write, "Theologically, nothing can separate us from the love of God in Christ Jesus our Lord; yet too many communities, even worshiping communities, have allowed themselves to be defined by sinful conceptions of personhood in ways that marginalize and isolate people in need. Ecclesially, there are far too many things that separate people from experiencing the love of God in Christ Jesus that ought to be expressed by the caregiving of others but often is not."[2]

Regular visitation not only helps to keep the older adults connected to the church, it also helps them to keep connected with God. But this poses some unique challenges because many pastors do not have the time to visit all their shut-ins. This is especially true if there are a lot of older adults in their congregations. One of the ways to overcome this challenge is for the church to train elders, deacons, and visitation committees to assist the pastor.

In Acts 14:23 we read that Paul and Barnabas *"appointed elders for them in every church, with prayer and fasting they committed them to the Lord in whom they had believed."* When we read this in context, we note that Paul and Barnabas appointed these elders in churches in Lystra, Iconium, and Antioch because they were going on to other cities. These elders were appointed by Paul and Barnabas to preach, teach, and carry on their ministry.

In 1 Timothy 5:17 Paul writes, *"Let the elders who rule well be considered worthy of double honor, especially those who labor in preaching and teaching."* James 5:14 says, *"Is anyone among you sick? Let him call for the elders of the church, and let them pray over him, anointing him with oil in the name of the Lord."* And Peter writes in 1 Peter 5:1-2a, *"So I exhort the elders among you, as a fellow elder and a witness of the sufferings of Christ, as well as a partaker in the glory that is going to be revealed: shepherd the flock of God that is among you."* These scriptures reveal to us the ministry of elders in the church—teach, preach, pray for the sick, and care for the flock. Regardless of what churches call their leadership—elders, deacons, councils, etc.—everyone involved in church leadership needs to be trained in how to visit, encourage, and care for the shut-ins.

I mentioned earlier that when I was a youngster, every family in our church received a visit from the elders every year. The elders teamed up in twos and spent about one hour visiting each family. They would make some small talk initially, then enquire about the welfare of each family member, read a scripture, and pray for us. These elders were trained to do that. The elders also assisted the pastor with visiting the church's shut-ins. Some churches also train lay people in visitation.

One of the things to keep in mind is that the same people should visit the same shut-ins in order to establish lasting and close relationships and in order to develop trust, which is necessary for shut-ins to share their feelings, hurts, fears, and concerns from the heart. It also enables them to observe any changes in the elderly person—both positive and negative changes. If negative changes are observed, the appropriate person could be notified—family, pastor, emergency services, and so on.

Affirming God's Love, Presence, and Forgiveness

How do we respond to the questions mentioned above that many older adults have concerning their faith and about God when they feel abandoned? These questions do not necessarily need to be answered individually. Rather, they need to be considered from a deeper need that many shut-ins have—the need for affirmation, validation, and assurance.

As a teenager, I often read Psalm 139. I had a huge inferiority complex, but I found great comfort in verses 13-18, *"For you formed my inward parts; you knitted me together in my mother's womb. I praise you, for I am fearfully and wonderfully made. Wonderful are your works; my soul knows it very well. My frame was not hidden from you, when I was being made in secret, intricately woven in the depths of the earth. Your eyes saw my unformed substance; in your book were written, every one of them, the days that were formed for me, when as yet there was none of them. How precious to me are your thoughts, O God! How vast is the sum of them! If I would count them, they are more than the sand. I awake, and I am still with you."* These words reassured me that God loved me; I never doubted that.

Yet at the same time, I was also afraid of God because of verses 1-5 and 7-9, *"O Lord, you have searched me and known me! You know when I sit down and when I rise up; you discern my thoughts from afar. You search out my path and my lying down and are acquainted with all my ways. Even before a word is on my tongue, behold, O Lord, you know it altogether. You hem me in, behind and before, and lay your hand upon me. ... Where shall I go from your Spirit? Or where shall I flee from your presence? If I ascend to heaven, you are there! If I make my bed in Sheol, you are there! If I take the wings of the morning and dwell in the uttermost parts of the sea ..."*

I would read these verses and be afraid of God. He knew everything about me—everything I did, everything I said, and even everything I thought. I felt hemmed in and trapped. I believed that since there was no place where I could hide from Him, sooner or later he would come looking for me and punish me for all my sinful deeds, words, and thoughts. Ironically, I knew God loved me, yet I was afraid of Him.

For some reason, I would also read verses 6 and 10, yet they didn't sink in. *"Such knowledge is too wonderful for me; it is high; I cannot attain it. ... even there your hand shall lead me, and your right hand shall hold me."* It was not until I was in my early twenties and a student at Elim Bible Institute and College in Lima, NY, that I began to realize that God's love for me and His thoughts about me resulted in His grace and mercy being poured out upon me and I did not have to be afraid of Him. I began to realize that the reason why I could not hide from God was so that he could find me whenever I went astray, and hold me close to His heart enabling me to feel His heartbeat of love for me, and gently guide me back on the right path.

My feelings as a teenager are similar to what many older adults feel, especially if they grew up in a legalistic church environment that gave them long lists of things they could not do along with a list of things they had to do. Is God now punishing them for their "sins" of not obeying church law? Often their "sins" were defined by what their church said were sins; a list that is almost Pharisaical—man-made rules that go way beyond the intent of scripture. Unfortunately, many of these same older adults have difficulty in feeling God's heartbeat of love as he holds them in His hands. They still need the affirmation of that love, which can only come through the church.

This may also present an opportunity to talk about eternal salvation, grace, and the hope we have in Christ. Religious legalism has a way of emphasizing salvation through works instead of grace. Ephesians 2:8 says, *"For by grace you have been saved through faith. And this is not your own doing; it is the gift of God."* Many life-long church attenders may never have had a personal relationship with Christ because they focused on obeying church law instead getting to know Christ as their Savior and Lord.

Along with this affirmation, they also need the assurance that their sins are forgiven. Many older adults have haunting memories of things they wish they could do over. They don't think about them until they are lonely with nothing to do accept to reminisce about the past. This assurance of the forgiveness of sin does not come from making amends, restitution, indulgences, or any other "works" because nothing we can do is good enough. The assurance of forgiveness can only come from scripture and sometimes by absolution, or pardon, from the church. Let me give you an example of what I mean.

Bill, a pastor friend of mine, felt that he had let a neighbor down when the neighbor's family member committed suicide. Bill could not overcome this feeling of guilt. He openly confessed this one time at an ecumenical Good Friday worship service. Another pastor stepped up and in front of the entire congregation said, "In the name of Jesus, I forgive you." It was as if Jesus Himself had spoken these words. Bill immediately felt peace and release from guilt.

I saw something similar happen with Jane who was afraid that God was going to punish her. She did not have the assurance of the forgiveness of sin. I had visited her on several occasions, each time showing her from scripture that her sins were forgiven. Each visit helped momentarily, but not for long. One day, I received a call from the nurse asking if I could visit Jane again. This time, I decided to try granting her absolution, which is not typically done in my faith tradition. I began by reading scripture reassuring her of her salvation and the forgiveness of sin. Then I asked her, "Do you believe in Jesus Christ as your Savior and Lord?" "Yes," she said. "Have you asked Him to forgive you of all your sins?"

"Yes." Then I responded, "By your confession and the promises of scripture, in the name of Jesus Christ, I forgive you of all your sins." From that point on, Jane had peace and assurance of her salvation and forgiveness.

God loves us for who we are, not for what we do. Unfortunately, people who grow up in a legalistic faith environment often base God's love on what they do. They need to be validated in the fact that they are God's children. We are all God's children by birth because we were created by Him in His image. But Paul makes a distinction between being a child of God through birth and being a child of God through faith. He says in Romans 9:8, *"This means that it is not the children of the flesh who are the children of God, but the children of the promise are counted as offspring."* He also says in Romans 8:14-16, *"For all who are led by the Spirit of God are sons of God. For you did not receive the spirit of slavery to fall back into fear, but you have received the Spirit of adoption as sons, by whom we cry, 'Abba! Father! The Spirit Himself bears witness with our spirit that we are children of God."* Paul also adds in Galatians 3:26, *"For in Christ Jesus you are all sons of God, through faith."*

It is also important to keep in mind that the need for forgiveness may reach beyond God's forgiveness of sins. There might be the need for the older adult to be forgiven by someone whom they have hurt, especially if they have an estranged son or daughter with whom they want to be reconciled before they die. Or they may need to forgive someone who hurt them and against whom they hold bitterness or anger. In either situation, you might still be able to grant them absolution similar to what I did in order for them to feel God's forgiveness. And if they want to be reconciled, you may need to contact the other person. Unfortunately, this might not always work, especially if the other person harbors a grudge and does not want reconciliation. One of the saddest funerals I did was for a man who held a grudge against his children. He was so bitter about what his children had done he did not even want them to know that he had died. There was no obituary in the paper and the only people at his funeral were his second wife, who was not the mother of his children, and a few close friends.

There might also be a need to forgive God. Many people think that it is a sin to be angry at God. Personally, I don't believe that. I have been angry at God on a number of occasions, even raising my fist into the air in anger towards Him once. We may be angry at God for a variety of reasons. Perhaps we experienced a terrible tragedy, or we feel he has abandoned us, or he didn't answer our prayers the way we expected, etc. God understands our anger, and when we come to Him in true repentance, he forgives us. One way that we can help someone forgive God is by reminding them that *"for those who love God all things work together for good, for those who are called according to His purpose."* (Romans 8:28). We might not always be able to see how things work for our good, so sometimes we need to engage the person in conversation and point out how God used those things for their good, or for the good of someone else. We may never see the good this side of heaven, and we need to simply have faith that God in His love for us allowed it to happen for whatever reason, and that through our suffering, he is somehow glorified.

Older adults, especially those who are shut-in or in a healthcare facility, have many unique needs caused by isolation, abandonment, loneliness, depression, failing health, numerous losses, and so on. Unless the church reaches out to them, those needs will not be met. The church has a biblical mandate to care for them.

Chapter 3:

Meeting the Needs of Older Adults

Making the Visit Meaningful

When I first became a long-term health care chaplain, I often felt uncomfortable in visiting the shut-ins on our two campuses. One reason for that is because I have always considered myself to be an introvert and was not very good at starting a conversation. However, over the years, I have become more extroverted and learned, often by trial and error, some ways to engage them in meaningful conversations.

Engaging the older adult in conversation is very important to their self-esteem, especially if the conversation revolves around them. Older adults love to reminisce so finding common ground enables them to do that because it indicates that you are also knowledgeable about the topic and that it is a topic important to you. For example, if your occupation is similar to theirs then you have common ground. And if they are considerably older than you, you can discuss the differences in the way things were done then as to how things are done now. Another way to engage them in conversation is to look around the room for conversation starters: knickknacks, family photos, souvenirs, and other sentimental mementos.

Keep in mind though that your objective is to engage them in the conversation. If your visit is to be meaningful for them, it has to be two-sided with you allowing the person to speak according to their ability to respond verbally. Remember that your role is to affirm and validate the shut-in, not yourself. David Kessler writes, "We often don't listen to their stories because ... we look at the outer shell rather than the inner spirit. Listening to the stories of the dying brings out their dignity and humanity."[1] We shouldn't wait until they are dying, we should do this with anyone who is shut-in and lonely.

If the person is no longer able to attend church, then if possible, bring a CD of the entire worship service with you when you visit; or perhaps view the service online or on your phone. My mother had rheumatoid arthritis which made it difficult for her to attend church in wintry weather so she would sometimes go for long periods of not attending the Sunday service. Someone would frequently drop off an audio recording of the sermon to which she could listen on her own during the week. But with all the new technology today, many older adults do not know how to use the equipment that would enable them to listen to or watch an audio or video recording. They may also not be able to access the sermon from the church's website. So, I would like to suggest that whoever brings the shut-in a recording of the sermon, stay with them and help them operate whatever device is used to listen to it.

Furthermore, I would also suggest that it be a video, not just an audio, recording. And, if the church is going to record the sermon, why not record the entire service if music copyrights allow? How much more meaningful would it be for the visitor to bring a video of the entire service complete with hymns, worship, and prayers, and play it for the shut-in; and also sing and worship along with the shut-in? If copyrights do not allow the recording of the entire service, the visitor could bring a hymn book and sing some favorite hymns together. The visitor should not worry about their singing ability; the shut-in will appreciate the fact that they want to help them experience as close to a worship service as possible. The shut-in will get much more out of that than simply listening to an audio recording of the sermon while sitting alone by themselves.

Holy Communion

Another important aspect of visitation is the sacrament of Holy Communion. "Most particularly, the Eucharist is a sacrament of hope that is crucial for all of us, and especially the elderly, as a reminder that our lives are not bounded by death but by the resurrected and resurrecting Christ."[2]

Some churches commission Eucharistic ministers whose primary responsibility is to bring the sacrament to the church's shut-ins, regardless of whether the shut-in lives at home or in a nursing facility. So how often should they be brought the sacrament? My suggestion is at least once a month. For churches that have Holy Communion every week, it might not be realistic to bring the sacrament to all their shut-ins every week. For churches that have Holy Communion once per quarter, that might be too long of a time lapse for shut-ins who have memory issues.

My dad was in a church related nursing home for several years before he passed away. He did not have dementia, although some of the residents did. I asked his chaplain how often he served Holy Communion to the dementia residents and his response floored me. He said, "Once a year, because they don't remember it." That denomination only served Holy Communion once a quarter. Every three months they brought one-fourth of the dementia residents to the Sunday chapel service so over the course of a year, all their dementia residents received Holy Communion once. It was obvious to me that the main reason why the residents didn't remember was that there was no consistency and continuity in ministry to these residents. Anyone who has worked with dementia patients for any length of time will tell you that consistency and continuity are important to their well-being.

At one of the facilities I worked, we did a brief worship service every week on all of our dementia units. We sang the old familiar hymns and served Holy Communion to everyone who had a church connection regardless of their denomination. Alzheimer's residents no longer made a distinction between denominations but they often remembered all or part of the old familiar hymns, all or part of the Lord's Prayer, and they also remembered the sacrament. They may not have remembered the significance of the sacrament, but they often remembered the ritual. The more frequently they received it, the better they remembered it.

Peter was a Roman Catholic and had mid-stage Alzheimer's. He could no longer speak but was able to communicate with facial expressions. His wife told me she only wanted him to receive Holy Communion from the Catholic Church and his facial expression indicated the same. However, he joined us for our weekly worship services on his unit, but I would pass him by when I served the sacrament. But after a few months as Peter's dementia worsened, I noticed that his facial expressions changed. Whenever I would pass him by, he would give me that "Why can't I have it?" look. When I mentioned this change in behavior to his wife, she realized that he no longer differentiated between Catholic and Protestant but still recognized the sacrament, so she gave me permission to give it to him, which made him happy.

Gloria would take the Communion wafer out of her mouth whenever I gave it to her. She would crumble it up and throw it down. After a while, I started questioning myself about giving it to her because it appeared that she no longer understood anything about the sacrament. But I would rather err on the side of grace than legalism so I continued to give it to her. One day, after I had finished serving Holy Communion to everyone present, she waved for me to come over. When I approached, she shook my hand and then crossed herself. I looked all over for the crumbled-up wafer but could not find it. It was not on her lap, not on her wheelchair, not on the floor; nowhere. I realized that she understood what she had received and wanted me to know that, but being non-verbal she used body language to communicate this to me. Unfortunately, Gloria died a week later.

But I had the joy of knowing that before she died, she understood what she received.

Any time we give the sacrament, we must do so without judgment. Whenever a new resident was admitted into our Skilled Nursing units, we would do a spiritual assessment to determine how we could best meet their spiritual needs. On my first visit with Susan, I asked her if she would like to receive Holy Communion. She said, "I can't. I am divorced." Her denominational background forbade her receiving the sacrament because she was divorced. I told her that I did not see that anywhere in scripture. She said, "You mean I can have Holy Communion?" When I said "yes," she broke down in tears of joy and said, "I have not had Holy Communion in thirty years."

Don't assume that if the person is in a church related nursing home that has a chaplain, that the chaplain will bring Holy Communion to all the residents every week or even every month. That was one of my goals when I first started as a nursing home chaplain, but no matter how hard I tried, it was not realistic. Too many other responsibilities prevented me from doing this on a regular basis. It is also important to remember that some denominations will only give the sacrament to residents of their own denomination; this includes certain Protestant denominations as well as the Roman Catholic and Orthodox churches. So, the chaplain might not give the sacrament to those of other denominations. I knew an Orthodox chaplain at another nursing home who would only give Holy Communion to Orthodox residents. So, his non-Orthodox residents did not receive Holy Communion unless someone from their own church brought it to them.

Before I leave the topic of Holy Communion, there is another story I want to share with you. I was in one of our Assisted Living units one day during Holy Week when I met a pastor who asked me for the room number of one of his parishioners because he wanted to bring the sacrament to all of his shut-ins during Holy Week. I responded, "She moved over to one of our Skilled

Nursing units fifteen months ago." Where was he all this time? His predecessor came to our campus every month to visit his shut-ins and offer them Holy Communion, but when he retired, his successor basically ignored them. Neither was there anyone in the church trained to assist the pastor with visitation.

Visitation should also include a scripture reading and prayer. As much as the visit will contain a large social element to it, you are also representing the church and even more importantly, you are going as an ambassador of Jesus Christ to bring Christ's love and presence into the shut-in's life. M. Therese Lysaught reminds us that "... the Christian community needs to attend to the fears, diminishment, and grief that accompany the losses and illnesses of aging, praying for the specific needs of those in their midst. Related sacramental activities, such as commissioning ministers to bring Communion to the sick and shut-ins and the practice of anointing of the sick, are further acts whereby the community as ecclesia makes itself present to those who are separated."[3]

When Speech is No Longer Possible

What about visiting older adults with Alzheimer's or other forms of dementia, including strokes or traumatic brain injuries? Unfortunately, many family members have difficulty visiting a loved one with dementia for a variety of reasons. "She is not the same person anymore." "He doesn't know who I am." "She won't remember my visit five minutes after I leave." "He is always mean and nasty when I visit." These might be truthful statements, but they are not good excuses for not visiting.

I remember Wendy, a resident who was in her fifties and had had a stroke in her brain stem. She was very cognitive but her only form of communication was to look up to say "yes" and to look down to say "no." As I got to know her over time, I felt comfortable enough to ask her some very personal yes/no questions. I discovered that she was disappointed in her daughter because her daughter worked at our facility but rarely visited her mother. She only visited on special occasions such as birthdays or holidays even though she was there every day for work. When I asked the daughter about that, she said, "It hurts too much to see my mother that way." Yet, she couldn't grasp how much she hurt her mother by not visiting.

I also discovered that even though Wendy's husband visited quite often after work in the evenings, she did not enjoy his visits. The resident sat propped up in bed and the TV was mounted on the wall opposite her so that she could watch it. The husband would bring in videos for himself to watch while he sat on a chair beside her bed. But her husband would just sit there without talking to her and he always watched violent, blood and guts videos which she did not like. She had no way to communicate her feelings to him because he never asked her. I offered to talk to him about it but she declined because Wendy didn't want to hurt his feelings; so, she just suffered in silence.

Communication is key, even with those who can't communicate either because of dementia or physical impairment. As in this story above, asking a yes/no question is one of the most effective ways to communicate with people who are cognitive but can't speak. Instead of asking an open-ended question such as, "How are you," ask "Are you fine?" Or instead of, "What would you like to watch on TV," ask, "Would you like to watch (state the name of a program)?" In the story above, the resident used her eyes to answer the questions. Other forms of response might be a shake or nod of the head. It might be one or two eye blinks, or one or two finger squeezes.

A letter and number board is another method which can be used and they are easy to make. On an 8.5x11 piece of card stock, write all the letters of the alphabet and the numbers 0 to 9. Then point to each letter or number and have the resident indicate which word he/she wants to spell out. This is a slow process, but effective. See the Addendum for a sample board.

Another good form of communication is to sing. When I first started working with dementia residents, I found out through trial and error what did or did not work. I am not a good singer and was somewhat self-conscious about that, especially singing solo in public. One day, I decided to sing to Mabel, a dementia resident who was lying in bed, flat on her back. She was babbling gibberish nonstop. I pulled up a chair and sang "Jesus Loves Me" and several other familiar hymns. After the third hymn, she stopped babbling and lay quietly listening as I sang a few more hymns. When I got up to leave, Mabel took my hand and spoke two syllables in gibberish. The intonation was the same intonation that we normally use when we say "Thank you." From that day on, I never let my poor singing stop me because I saw the effect that singing has on dementia residents. In fact, I copied a lot of familiar hymns in small font onto small pieces of paper and carried them in my shirt pocket so they were always available.

We can also engage in what is referred to as a ministry of presence. A beautiful example of this is in the book of Job. Job was suffering all by himself, sitting on the ash heap covered in boils, and also grieving the loss of his family, his servants, and his livestock. After a while, three friends went and sat with him in silence. Their silent presence comforted Job. Job 2:13 says, *"And they sat with him on the ground seven days and seven nights, and no one spoke a word to him, for they saw that his suffering was very great."* Unfortunately, they eventually started talking and started accusing Job of all kinds of things which only made his suffering worse. But, their initial week of silence brought Job comfort because he was no longer grieving alone. Kessler writes, "It's okay just to be with them without saying anything. The point is to be there for them."[4]

One of my most cherished memories is of Tony who had dementia, couldn't speak, and couldn't remember what he ate for lunch. I had the privilege of being on his dementia unit on a number of occasions when his wife came to visit him. As soon as he saw her walking down the hall, his face immediately brightened up with a huge smile and a look of love coming from his eyes. He may not have been able to communicate verbally, but her presence brought him great joy.

A key component of meaningful communication is to not give up. Many of the above suggestions I learned through consulting with others or through trial and error. When new residents came to us, they were strangers to us and we didn't know anything about them—their likes and dislikes, their needs, their spiritual journey, their families, etc. We had to learn how to be creative and try different methods of communication until we found what worked. One advantage to ministering to the elderly in your church is that you may have already established a relationship with them, so you might have a place from which to start; whereas we had to start from scratch. However, as their health declines, their needs change and so might their method of communication. When one method no longer works, try another, and another, and another until you find one that works. But, don't give up; they need you.

There are also other things that can be done during visitation such as playing cards or board games, or assembling jig-saw puzzles, etc. With some creativity they could be given simple things to do to make them feel useful and needed. Perhaps they can assist in helping stuff envelopes for church mailings. Or they could become prayer warriors and be brought prayer lists or missionary newsletters. They might be able to become pen pals with missionaries or write get well cards to the sick. With some imagination in giving them small projects to do, they can keep their dignity and self-worth.

Chapter 4:

Elderly Prodigals

Proverbs 22:6 says, *"Train up a child in the way he should go; even when he is old, he will not depart from it."* Personally, I find this scripture to be so full of promise for those believers who appear to go astray. They stop going to church for whatever reason, their lifestyle as a "Christian" is questionable, they think that all Christians are hypocrites, or they are angry at God. There are a million and one reasons why they appear to have lost the faith, why they have become "prodigal" Christians. The reason why I find this promise so reassuring is because I have seen so many older adults return to the faith as their health declines. When they lose their independence, experience pain, are unable to function as well as they once could, and face their own immortality, they frequently start to become more spiritual and turn back to God.

Hurt Caused by the Church

Steve had left the church because of all the sexual scandals making the news. He wasn't sure anymore if God even existed. Rather than condemning or judging him for his feelings and loss of faith, I affirmed his right to feel that way. This opened the door for several conversations about God and faith to the point where I was able to challenge him to really think about his faith. To my complete surprise, one day Steve came to a chapel service. After the service, I asked him why he had come. With tears of joy running down his face and with a smile from ear to ear, he said, "He saved me." I said, "What do you mean; who saved you?" Pointing upward, he emphatically responded, "You know, he saved me." We didn't have time to go into a detailed conversation then, and unfortunately, we never had that opportunity because he unexpectedly died a few days later. But I knew that somehow as Steve was alone in his room, he came to salvation. Had I not affirmed his right to be angry at the church and question God's existence, or had I condemned him for the way he felt, I would never have been able to have had those other conversations with him which led to his salvation and peace with God.

Jill, one of our employees, told me that her mother Pauline was coming into our facility. Jill also told me that her mother would not like me because she had had a run-in with her pastor many years ago and had left the church. My first encounter with Pauline was shortly after she was admitted and Jill was wheeling her down the hall; Jill gave us a formal introduction. Pauline only had a few months to live so I made it a point to visit her as often as possible. The first few visits were strictly social. I did not do any spiritual ministry because my initial goal was just to build a relationship with her. After several visits, Pauline asked me to pray the Lord's prayer with her. After a few more visits, she requested Holy Communion. Little by little, I saw her faith return. We never discussed why she had left the church. I never condemned her or judged her for having left. I simply identified with her level of faith and accepted her as a person.

When Pauline died, Jill asked me to do a graveside service for her. Jill was a very devout Christian so I questioned her as to why she wanted me to do the service instead of a pastor. Jill said it was because I had brought her mother back to faith. I told Jill that her mother's faith was there all the time, just buried under a lot of hurt. To which Jill responded, "Well, you brought it out of her." I answered, "No, I did not. The Holy Spirit did." Jill replied, "Well, you were the conduit of the Holy Spirit." Seeing that I wasn't getting anywhere with Jill, I relented and did the graveside service.

In both Steve and Pauline's cases, and I suspect the same is true for many people who have left the church, their faith was still there. However, because of the hurts they experienced by the church, their faith became buried under layers of pain; even to the point where it appeared they had lost their faith. But, love and acceptance without judgment helped to peel back each layer of pain until their faith in God, although not necessarily the church, became visible again.

Receiving the Prodigal

In the story of the Prodigal Son in Luke 15, the younger brother left the family home. However, his father looked down the road every day for the son to return. Verse 20b states *"But while he was still a long way off, his father saw him and felt compassion, and ran and embraced him and kissed him."* Such is the promise of Proverbs 22:6; when given the opportunity, those who appear to have left the faith will return as they get older.

But what do I mean about given the opportunity? When those who leave the family of God decide to return, the Father runs to them, embraces them, and kisses them. But all too often, the church acts like the older brother, finds fault with them for having left, and refuses to embrace and kiss them. When we refuse to accept them as they are, dirty and smelly from the pig pen, we are not giving them the opportunity to return to the faith. With both Steve and Pauline, there was no judgment and no condemnation by any of our employees. There was full acceptance, we embraced them as they were, and they returned.

Do we as pastors, as lay leaders, and as a church have a responsibility to seek those who left the church? Yes, yes, yes. The good shepherd leaves the ninety-nine and searches for the one that was lost. Jesus made that very clear in Luke 15:3-6.

Matthew 25:34-46 gives us a very sobering warning by Jesus to care for others. *"Then the King will say to those on his right, 'Come, you who are blessed by my Father, inherit the kingdom prepared for you from the foundation of the world. For I was hungry and you gave me food, I was thirsty and you gave me drink, I was a stranger and you welcomed me, I was naked and you clothed me, I was sick and you visited me, I was in prison and you came to me.' Then the righteous will answer him, saying, 'Lord, when did we see you hungry and feed you, or thirsty and give you drink? And when did we see you a stranger and welcome you, or naked and clothe you? And when did we see you sick or in prison and visit you?' And the King will answer them, 'Truly, I say to you, as you did it to one of the least of these my brothers, you did it to me. Then he will say to those on his left, 'Depart from me, you cursed, into the eternal fire prepared for the devil and his angels. For I was hungry and you gave me no food, I was thirsty and you gave me no drink, I was a stranger and you did not welcome me, naked and you did not clothe me, sick and in prison and you did not visit me.' Then they also will answer, saying, 'Lord, when did we see you hungry or thirsty or a stranger or naked or sick or in prison, and did not minister to you?' Then he will answer them, saying, 'Truly, I say to you, as you did not do it to one of the least of these, you did not do it to me.' And these will go away into eternal punishment, but the righteous into eternal life."*

Are we to sit in our churches and wait for the hungry, the thirsty, the stranger, the naked, the sick, or the prisoner to come to us? No. They won't, or in some cases, they can't. We are to go to them. Neither are we to wait for the prodigals to return to the church. They won't, or in some cases, they can't. We have to go to them. But, how do we go to them? With an attitude of self-righteousness? With an attitude that says, "Come back, or else?" Absolutely not. We must search for them with a spirit of humility and meekness.

When I was a young pastor, I attended a conference which greatly impacted my ministry. The speaker commented that as a church leader, we are responsible for the actions of our predecessor and we must take their actions as our own if we are to minister forgiveness and reconciliation. A few years later, I had the opportunity to do exactly that as several former church members returned with horror stories of how my predecessor had treated them. Reconciliation was only obtained when I stood in place of my predecessor, humbled myself to these former parishioners, and asked for their forgiveness.

We have a beautiful example of this in Daniel 9. Daniel recognized that the seventy-year captivity was about to end so with fasting, sackcloth, and ashes, he confessed the sins of his forefathers as his own saying, "We have sinned and done wrong and acted wickedly and rebelled, turning aside from your commandments and rules." (verse 5). Daniel was a righteous person fully devoted to serving God. Yet, in his prayer he said "we" instead of "our forefathers."

The only way that those who have left the church for whatever reason will return is for us as a church and as ministry leaders to humble ourselves and confess the sins of the church to those who have been hurt by the church. We must listen to their story without judgment or condemnation asking them for forgiveness and recognizing that only then can their pain be healed and reconciliation be obtained. Even if they are not reconciled back to the church, the door is open for them to be reconciled back to God. This is especially relevant for those who grew up in legalistic churches and feel betrayed because their church leaders did exactly what they taught the congregation not to do. Humbling ourselves to those who have been hurt opens the door for God's grace to flow into their lives. And grace opens the heart to receive forgiveness and reconciliation.

I realize that this won't necessarily apply to the elderly shut-ins in your church, although it might. However, if you visit them in nursing homes, you will invariably meet and get to know other residents and some of them may be "prodigals." Even though they may not have been members of your congregation, use these opportunities to minister God's love, acceptance, and forgiveness to them. Remember, we are called to minister to the whole body of Christ, not just those of our congregation.

Chapter 5:

Nursing Home Placement

My mother developed rheumatoid arthritis when she was in her late twenties. Even though she fought hard against the disease, she was in a wheelchair by the time she was in her mid-fifties. By that time, my sister, brother, and I had all left home so my dad was her sole caregiver for many years. Several years after dad retired, they moved into a Continuum Care Retirement Center (CCRC) that was affiliated with their church. They made this decision on their own because they realized that dad would not be able to care for mom as he got older.

After they had lived there for a number of years in Independent Living, dad needed to go to the hospital for about a week for surgery, so he moved mom into respite nursing care. During that week, he asked me to tell mom that she would have to remain in the Nursing unit permanently because he was no longer able to care for her. When I told her, she became very upset and asked me why. She did not realize that dad's body could no longer meet her needs with dressing and undressing her, toileting her numerous times throughout the day and night, preparing meals, keeping their apartment clean, doing laundry, grocery shopping, etc. It wasn't that dad was not willing, but his body was also aging and wearing out.

So, I told her that if she went back to living in the apartment, I truly believed that dad would be dead within six months. However, if she agreed to permanent nursing care, I also believed that as dad's health recovered, she would be able to spend a considerable amount of time each day with him in their apartment. And that is exactly what happened. With dad being free from the responsibility of providing twenty-four hour care for her, his health recovered to the point where he was able to spend about an hour every morning with her on the Nursing unit. And after lunch, the nursing staff prepared mom to go to their apartment for the remainder of the day with her only needing minimum care from dad. This continued for several years until dad eventually needed nursing care himself. Mom even told me one time, "I still live up here, I only eat and sleep downstairs."

One of the things for which I was extremely grateful was that my parents made all these decisions on their own. They jointly decided to move into a CCRC. Dad also decided when it was time for mom and when it was time for himself to go into nursing care. This took a huge weight from off my siblings and me.

We had a slightly different situation with my mother-in-law. She eventually came to live with us, but as her health continued to decline, we had to hire a private duty aide to be with her while my wife and I worked or if we had to go somewhere. Over time, this became more and more of an issue. At one point she said to us, "Maybe it is time for me to go into nursing care." We told her that we would keep her at home with us for as long as possible; which we did. But several months later, when she began to require twenty-four hour care, and sometimes with the assist of two, we put her into one of the nursing homes where I worked. My wife also worked there so we were still able to spend some time with her almost every day.

Notice that we did not tell her, "We will never put you into a nursing home." We said that we would keep her at our home for as long as possible. Many families have an unrealistic understanding of how much care their loved ones might need. And if their care is more than the family is capable of providing, the family feels guilty about placing their loved one into a nursing facility. And often, their loved one reminds them of that promise they had made and puts a guilt trip on the family. I have seen families devastated by guilt and I have seen residents angry at their children simply because the children had made this unrealistic promise.

Choosing a Care Facility

As a church leader, you most likely will be ministering to families that need to make some difficult age-related decisions. The following suggestions will be helpful.

If it comes to the point where an older adult requires twenty-four hour nursing care, either because of dementia or because of declining physical health, how does the family decide where to place their loved one?

I have often counseled families not to wait until the last minute. If their loved one should happen to fall at home and fracture a hip, or if their loved one has a stroke or other medical emergency, then when he/she is discharged from the hospital, he/she might not be able to return home. This puts the family into the awkward position of having to make an immediate decision as to where to place their loved one. Not all nursing homes are the same, not all provide the same kind of care or level of care so the facility might not be a good match for the person.

My advice is to shop around before a nursing facility is needed and make an informed decision ahead of time so that if nursing care is required, the choice will have already been made. The same is true if Alzheimer's or some other form of dementia is beginning to present itself. Some memory care facilities offer day care which can be a huge benefit for two reasons. First, it gives the family some respite for a few hours several times a week. Second, it acclimates their loved one to being in a care facility.

In choosing a nursing or memory care facility, one good place to start is the internet. Medicare has a rating system based on annual inspections that are done by the state. Go to www.medicare.gov/nursinghomecompare and enter your zip code. This will give you a list of nursing homes in your area and the star ratings given to them by Medicare.

Another resource is your state's department that oversees nursing homes. By going onto their website, you should be able to find annual survey/inspection reports for nursing homes in your area. One thing to keep in mind is that in many cases, if a facility gets a negative survey, it is usually the result of insufficient documentation, not in actual care provided by staff. Reports from your county's Ombudsman, Agency on Aging, and Protective Services are also reliable sources to obtain information on nursing homes.

Then there is also word of mouth. If you know of other families who have loved ones in a nursing facility, ask them about their experiences. You should also call ahead and request to tour local nursing homes. When doing so, don't just talk to your tour guide, but also ask questions of residents and staff about the care, activities, and amenities that they provide. Remember, you want to gain as much knowledge about the nursing home as possible so that you can make an informed decision if one is needed later on.

Artificial Life Support

Many nursing homes require you to sign an end-of-life document stating what care is desired if the older adult is nearing death. This is one of the most challenging questions often faced with the care for the elderly. Do they want CPR if they stop breathing or their heart stops beating? Do they want a feeding tube if they are no longer able to eat or swallow? Do they want to be put on a ventilator or respirator if breathing on their own becomes too difficult to sustain life? Written documentation to answer these or other life or death questions is very helpful to both family and staff. Although it must be recognized that these wishes might not always be followed, they provide a good starting point for families to come to an agreement beforehand should these situations arrive.

But how should these situations be resolved if the older adult was put on these artificial life supports expecting it to be temporary only to discover later on that life cannot be sustained if these supports are removed? Such was the case with Jack. His wife was put on life support with the expectation that it would only be necessary for a few months. But as the months dragged on into years she remained in a comatose state. Jack told me that if they had known this was going to be the result, neither of them would have accepted artificial life support; they would have allowed her to die a natural death. However, since she was on them, Jack did not have the heart to remove these supports. He viewed that as murder. Jack was not the only case we have had over the years. His case was one of many similar situations that we encountered.

As a pastor or lay leader in your church, how would you respond if this was one of your parishioners, especially if this was dividing the family and causing tension between family members? All you can do is to provide some guidance but recognize that whatever decision the family makes, your role is to remain neutral and support all family members.

My personal view is that any artificial means of life support is exactly what it says—artificial, not natural. There are a lot of short-term benefits to these support systems, but it is my opinion that they do not prolong life; they simply prolong the agonizing process of dying. In some cases, it could be physically painful for the residents, but in most cases, it is unbearably emotionally stressful for the family. I am not a proponent of using medical science to speed up the process of dying, but neither am I a proponent of using medical science to slow down the inevitable.

Kessler agrees stating, "Is there a midpoint between forcing people to accept painful care they wish to avoid and letting them die from lack of care? We want people to die naturally, but is it natural to be kept 'alive' in a coma on a respirator with zero brain functioning for years, receiving predigested amino acids through a nasal tube into the stomach? Something has gone wrong with the medical community when it refers to withdrawing artificial technological support, feeding tubes, and respirators as 'killing' our loved ones. In some cases, technology does nothing more than increase the length and depth of suffering at the end of life. ... But if quality of life is considered at all, there may be a time to say no. We must find ways to decrease the suffering brought about by technology. We must learn to make the distinction between ending suffering and ending life."[1]

I recognize that not everyone who reads this will agree on this matter, but our role in caring for the elderly and their families is not to coerce or force our opinions on them. We certainly have the right to voice our views out of loving concern, but in the end, the decision is theirs and we need to support them in it without judgment or condemnation. I have supported and prayed with residents and families who were emotionally unable to end artificial means of life support, and I have also stood by the bedside praying for and supporting residents and their families as life support was discontinued.

This is where we hold on to the hope and the promise of eternal life for those who put their faith and trust in Jesus Christ as Savior and Lord. Either way, we enable the dying person to die with dignity, releasing them into the loving arms of Jesus.

Chapter 6:

The Needs of the Dying

About one or two years after I became a long-term health care chaplain, I was feeling a little discouraged. Some of the other pastors in our community were reporting at our monthly ministerial meetings on how their churches were growing. I felt a little bit jealous and was bemoaning the fact that all my "parishioners" were dying. Our census remained the same month after month. As soon as a resident died, a new resident moved in. But our numbers never grew.

I never told anyone how I was feeling, but God sent Bill, my pastor friend whom I mentioned in Chapter 2, to help me change my attitude. He made an unsolicited and unexpected comment to me. Bill said, "You know John, you are so blessed to have the privilege to be with people as they are dying and being with them as they enter heaven." I had never considered this aspect before—that it was a privilege to be with them and help them through this transition. Between the two large nursing facilities where I worked, we averaged about fifteen to twenty deaths per month. Sharing the load with two other chaplains, and with many of our residents having their own pastors, I was not physically present with each resident at the exact time of death and I did not personally minister to each one as they were dying. But death and dying was always on the minds of most of our residents so this would frequently come up in discussions with them or their families.

Some of our residents looked forward to death. For them, death would bring relief from a lot of pain and suffering, from being bedfast, isolated, depressed, etc. And for those who were strong in faith with full assurance of eternal life, knowing that death was imminent brought great peace. It was always a joy to spend time with them as they were dying. Phyllis was slowly dying and in constant pain. But every time I went to see her, she wanted me to grab a hymn book and the two of us would sing hymns for a while. I always left feeling that she ministered to me rather than me to her.

Fear of Death

For other residents, especially those who came from a legalistic faith environment, there was always the concern of not being good enough. For them it was important that they received assurance from scripture and perhaps also receiving absolution (see chapter 2).

But I discovered that when a resident told me that they were afraid of dying, I would have to ask them what they meant. Were they afraid of death itself, not certain of where they would spend eternity? Or, were they afraid of the process of dying, how much pain and suffering they would experience, how long it might take, were they going to die alone, etc.? Cloutier writes, "The elderly in our society are often faced with two rather overwhelming fears: the fear of becoming a burden and the fear of a lingering, painful death."[1] Sometimes it wasn't the resident asking these questions, but their families.

The fear of a lingering, painful death, or the fear of dying alone, must not be overlooked, although it often is. One of the two facilities where I used to work was a Continuum Care Retirement Community (CCRC) so our residents ranged from fairly healthy residents who were totally independent, to residents who required twenty-four hour Skilled Nursing care. Many of our independent residents felt extremely uncomfortable when it came to visiting those in Skilled Nursing because "someday it might be me." They didn't want to face their own mortality and the end-of-life suffering they might experience.

Shuman writes, "The distorted and altogether circular logic of the relationship between aging and death in our culture is this:

Because we know that it is old people who most often die, we fear becoming old or being long in the presence of those who are old, for we fear death. But one of the reasons we fear death is that we have no sense or experience of what it might mean for us or someone else to have a good death. And we have no sense or experience of what it might mean to have a good death in part because we have separated ourselves from those who are in the processes of dying—usually the elderly—by allowing them to be placed in institutions and cared for by professionals, often long before death comes. Their deaths are frequently unnecessarily protracted, lonely, and miserable; we know (or at least we suspect) this, and so we stay away from them, because we fear seeing ourselves and our own deaths reflected back to us in their eyes."[2]

Dying a Good Death

But what does Shuman mean by "a good death?" Kessler writes, "The dying want to be treated—and they have the need to be treated—as living human beings until the moment they die. But often we 'bury them alive' by thinking of them as their diseases, by acting as if they are incapable of making their own decisions, by negating their opinions, by overlooking their desires, by withholding information from them, and by omitting them from conversations. Without realizing we are doing so, we rob them of their dignity, we rob them of their hope, and we rob them of their very humanity."[3] So, a good death is one that guards their dignity, gives them hope, and affirms their humanity.

According to Kessler, "While we should never deny that the dying are dying, we should also never treat them as broken or no longer whole. Despite their illnesses, despite the fact that they are dying, they are still whole human beings. ... We must continue to see them as they see themselves, to listen to their stories, to support their hope, and to treat them with dignity."[4]

Kessler also states that, just like everybody else, the dying also have a need to hope. He says, "Hope should never go away, but what we hope for can change."[5] When there is no longer the medical possibility of restored or improved health, or the hope of reduced pain and suffering, or the hope of restoration of broken relationships, we have something else to which we can look forward. It is a hope that can give strength to the elderly, even as death approaches and we think that "all hope is gone." Kessler brings out a valid point that hope should never go away, instead we need to change for what we hope. For the believer, there is the sure and certain hope of the resurrection of the dead (see Romans 6:5; 1 Corinthians 15), so when all hope in this life is gone, we can redirect their hope towards eternity.

However, some people may question the strength of their faith and whether or not they deserve eternal life. But impending death is not a time of condemnation or judgment. These are times of reassurance, affirmation, and validation which can only be found in the Gospel. This presents a wonderful opportunity to share reassuring scriptures with them.

Letting Go

Sometimes, there is the need for family to give permission for the dying person to die. This helps both the dying person and the family. Betty was in her mid-fifties and actively dying, but she seemed to linger needlessly long after the doctors had said she would. Her daughter Laura came in every day to visit her, often coming in the mornings and staying until evenings. Laura was extremely close to her mom and kept encouraging her to get well.

One morning, I walked into Betty's room and in a barely audible whisper she was saying, "I'm going. I'm going." She kept repeating this over and over again. Meanwhile, with tears in her eyes, Laura was practically in her mother's face with her mouth right next to Betty's ear and repeatedly saying, "Don't say that mom, you're not going." I asked Laura to step out in the hall with me and we talked about her need to let her mom go and to tell her that she had Laura's permission to go.

Later that afternoon, I ran into Laura in the hallway and she had a huge smile and peaceful look on her face. She turned to me and said, "I did it. I told my mom that she could go and now I feel like a huge weight has been lifted off my shoulders." Betty died later that evening. I have encountered many similar situations where a dying person lingered for days or even weeks because the family couldn't say good-bye, but once the family did so, within hours their loved one passed away.

There is a liturgical ritual which can help this. In the Roman Catholic church, it is called "The Anointing of the Sick," more commonly known as last rites. In the Lutheran church, it is called "A Commendation of the Dying." Some other denominations have similar rituals. Basically, these rituals affirm the forgiveness of sins, salvation through Christ, and eternal life. These rituals are also a means of giving permission for their loved one to pass away. Some families find great comfort in having these prayers read. While I am not suggesting that these prayers will result in a person's salvation, they often bring peace during a time of grieving and could possibly open the door for a future discussion on salvation with the dying person, the family, or both.

We also need to recognize that sometimes the dying person wants to die alone. It is quite common for family to keep a bedside vigil because they want to be there right up to the end. Yet, it is also not uncommon for the person to die when the family leaves the room for a few minutes. When the family returns and are informed that their loved one died moments ago, the family occasionally gets upset because they "missed it." However, we need to realize that sometimes the dying person doesn't want family to see them take their last breath.

It is also important to remember that even though a dying person appears to be asleep or is unresponsive, there is still the possibility that they can hear and understand what is being said.

So, this is not the time or place for families to discuss care and treatment. Some family members may want to do everything possible to prolong life while other family members may want to keep the person on comfort measures only. Any discussions on end-of-life care should be out of earshot of the dying person, especially if there is strong disagreement. The same is true about discussing funeral arrangements. The person hasn't died yet, they are still alive. Therefore, the dying person should be treated with respect with regards to what is discussed in their presence.

Grieving

In understanding the needs of the dying, it is also important to understand the grieving process. However, people grieve for many reasons, not just over the loss of a loved one. They grieve over the loss of mobility, functionality, possessions, health, relationships, jobs, and so on. Some also grieve about their impending death not wanting to say goodbye to their families.

However, regardless of why a person is grieving, the emotions experienced are the same. These emotions may include shock, denial, sadness, depression, anger, and guilt. They may come in any order or in repetitive stages. Or, they may not come at all.

When my mother died, my father repeatedly said, "I'm free. I'm free." My dad did not appear to grieve. I never asked him about this, but I thought about it later. I believe that he reacted this way because my mother had been confined to a wheelchair since her mid-fifties and my father was her primary caregiver for close to thirty years. I believe he had done all his grieving during those difficult years of caring for her. In that sense, he truly was free.

Another reason why some people don't grieve over the death of a spouse is if the spouse was verbally, mentally, or physically abusive. For them, their spouse's death is a relief and they are glad the abuse is over.

In ministering to those who are grieving, it is important to keep in mind that there is usually no wrong way to grieve IF they are moving on with life. A funeral director told me about a lady whom he knew who lost her dad when she was a teenager. Now in her thirties, she was still living at home with her mother. Her mother had never allowed her to date because they were grieving. Even now, years later her mother was still setting a place for him at the dinner table. This is not healthy grieving as the mother was not moving on and would not allow her daughter to move on.

It is not wise to tell the grieving person that time will heal his/her grief. That is not true. Only God can heal it. Also, time sometimes makes grief worse, especially for those who have become shut-in and are isolated and lonely. Their loneliness sometimes intensifies their grief.

So how do we help someone who is grieving, regardless if it is the person who is dying or the person's family?

- Give permission to grieve and accept his/her feelings.
- Help with necessary decisions and tasks.
- Use active listening and good communications skills.
- Be present, even silently.
- Give assurance that the emotions the person is experiencing are a normal part of the healing process and that things will improve.
- Help him/her to see that the death was not his/her fault.
- As an ambassador of Christ, manifest his compassionate, caring love.
- Dying is a normal part of living, but is never easy. However, understanding death, the process of dying, and grief, will enable you to minister Christ's love and presence to those experiencing it.

Chapter 7:

Developing a Team

In ministering to the elderly shut-ins, it is important for the church to realize that the pastor cannot do it alone. There are many demands put on the pastor which the church must recognize: sermon and Bible study preparation, hospital visits, elder's meetings, private counseling, and most importantly, safeguarding his personal relationship with Jesus Christ and meeting the needs of his/her family.

It takes an entire church to effectively minister to the elderly. So, how does the church do that? First, the church needs to understand that it already has all the resources needed—people. That's right. Ministry to the elderly only requires people, people who are committed to helping others. So, it is important that the pastor surrounds him/herself with a team that has a compassion to help others.

Composition of a Team

In chapter one, I mentioned that the church in which I grew up was divided into districts, one per elder, and that every autumn the elders teamed up in twos and visited every member within their two districts. These elders were trained how to do that.

In chapter two, I referred to a number of scriptures which indicate that Paul set up elders to assist the pastors. These elders were to assist in teaching, preaching, praying for the sick, and caring for the flock. So properly trained and commissioned elders make up the first line of those called upon to assist the pastor in ministering to the elderly.

But lay people can also be trained and commissioned to do this. One organization that can help to train lay people is called Stephen Ministries. This ministry, founded in 1975 by Dr. Kenneth C. Haugk, has trained approximately 700,000 pastors and lay leaders in how to provide one-on-one ministry to people who need care and support. To learn more, you can access their website at www.stephenministries.org.

At the CCRC facility mentioned in chapter four, the other chaplain and I developed two programs for volunteers. One program concentrated on visiting the shut-ins on our campus. Most of these shut-ins were confined to our Skilled Nursing and dementia units, although some were also in our Assisted Living section. The goal of this program was to provide socialization, encouragement, and support to those who were room or bed bound. The other program focused on sitting with those who were actively dying, if other family members or friends were not available, so that the dying person would not have to die alone. All these volunteers were trained using materials that we developed out of our own experiences and research. Most of the volunteers for these two programs were other residents who lived on the campus although some came from our staff or lived in the local community. Some of the training material that we developed has already been mentioned throughout this book. More information can be found in the Addendum following this chapter.

One excellent source for volunteers are the retirees in your church. Many retirees are looking for places to volunteer. They don't want to sit around all day with nothing to do. In many cases, they will already have formed friendships among the shut-ins, so it is not as if strangers were coming to visit them. They may already have a lot of things in common such as similar vocations, interests, hobbies, places they have visited, etc. But the retirees may need to be trained in how to provide spiritual care for the shut-ins since they would be making more than just social visits. They would be going as ambassadors of Jesus Christ.

Another benefit of asking retirees to join the ministry team is that they are in the same age group as the elderly shut-ins and understand the unique challenges experienced as one grows older. And in many cases, widows have a much better understanding of what it means to lose a spouse.

Small groups are another source of volunteers. Many churches today have home groups or small groups that are led by trained leaders. These groups may meet for Bible studies, discussions on the pastor's sermons, prayer meetings, or for a variety of other reasons. Because close relationships are developed over time within the small groups, they provide an excellent source of support when an elderly member experiences declining health.

One final area of ministry in which lay people can be trained is to bring Holy Communion to the shut-ins. The Roman Catholic church has specifically trained and commissioned lay people called Eucharistic Ministers who bring Holy Communion to parishioners confined to their own homes or in nursing homes. Some churches have policies that only an ordained minister can serve Holy Communion. However, I don't see that anywhere in Scripture. I respect the need for guidelines when it comes to serving the sacrament, but properly trained and commissioned lay people and/or the elders of a church could assist the pastor in providing this sacrament.

The importance of Holy Communion should not be overlooked, even for those with dementia. When conversation no longer meets the spiritual needs of those with dementia because they have lost the ability to comprehend things mentally, they usually still remember familiar rituals such as reciting the Lord's Prayer, singing old familiar hymns, and Holy Communion.

Caring for shut-ins is not the sole responsibility of the pastor. Simply put, most pastors do not have the time to visit every shut-in on a regular basis. The contributions that elderly shut-ins have made to the church in the past should not be overlooked. These people need to be honored, not forgotten. According to Leviticus 19:32 and James 1:27, the church has a mandate from

God to care for the elderly, the widowed, and the orphaned. It is great that many churches have programs staffed by trained volunteers to attract the youth. But we also need to have programs staffed by trained volunteers to minister to the elderly shut-ins so that they don't become God's Forgotten Pillars.

Benefits of Team Ministry

There are many benefits of team ministry, one of which is the fact that God has not equipped any individual person to be all things to all people. God has made us all uniquely different in order to meet all possible needs that arise. This was really brought home for me at the CCRC where I worked.

The other chaplain and I at first had separate offices and we each did our own thing. But after a number of years, Administration decided they needed my office for something else and I had to move my desk into the other chaplain's office. It took both of us some time to adjust to this change, but over time we began to get a clearer understanding of each other's and our own strengths and weaknesses. That is when we began to flow together as a team, each one of us giving precedence to the other when the other was better skilled in a certain area. But at the same time, we were able to help each other hone our skills in which we were weak.

Pastors need to surround themselves with men and women who have different skills, gifts, abilities, and personalities, and allow them to assist in ministry. Pastors also need to recognize those within their churches who have potential in ministry and then mentor them so they can reach their potential. If pastors don't have the skills to mentor others, they need to bring someone in who can train them in those areas, or help them find resources they can use to develop their potential.

When pastors are willing to humble themselves and admit that they need assistance, and when they are willing to train and mentor others to help them, the church will grow. This is true regardless of the area of ministry. Many churches already train others to oversee Sunday School or youth ministries. We also need to train people to minister to the needs of the elderly shut-ins.

It is impossible for me to include every conceivable need of older adults. However, as you have probably noticed, their needs are great. Many of them suffer from physical pain and discomfort, emotional stress due to numerous losses and uncertainties, and spiritual concerns about God's love and presence. They are part of the body of Christ, and as servant-leaders of Christ's body, we not only have a responsibility to minister to them, we have an obligation and a mandate from Jesus Christ Himself to do so.

Addendum

I have already given many practical suggestions for ministering to elderly shut-ins. The following offers further suggestions. These suggestions are primarily for visiting older adults in nursing homes or other health care facilities, but many of them are also applicable when visiting them in their own homes.

Confidentiality

It is important that every effort is made to protect the privacy of those you visit. Kent C. Miller writes, "Trust must not become a casualty or the ministry will be lost. Confidentiality is both a legal and ethical issue; it must be fully understood in most ministries of the church and certainly in a ministry to homebound persons."[1] Anything shared with you by those whom you visit is to be regarded as confidential. If it's something you would like to share with others, please ask permission before doing so.

However, if the person's health or safety is at risk, intervention may be necessary. Miller continues, "When the ministry team becomes aware of critical situations such as abuse (child abuse, elder abuse, spouse abuse, self abuse) or neglect (child or elder), they have both moral and legal reasons to report this."[2] Other reasons why reporting may be necessary include sexual abuse, family violence, financial mismanagement, alcohol or drug abuse, mental illness, and dementia.

If you notice that the elderly shut-in is at risk, you should notify the appropriate person—family member, pastor, the local Area Agency on Aging, or if there is an immediate emergency, call 911.

If the resident has a special problem which does not pose a risk but needs further attention, ask the resident if you can share it with an appropriate person.

Showing Respect

When visiting in a care facility, always knock before entering a room, even if the door is open. If the door is closed, the person may be sleeping or receiving care from staff, so knock and wait until you are invited to enter.

Address the person as Mr. or Mrs. unless you already have a close relationship with him/her. Also, tell him/her your name, especially if he/she doesn't know you or can't remember you. After your initial visit, feel free to ask him/her what name he/she would prefer that you use.

Safety Concerns

If the person you are visiting is in a wheelchair and you wish to take him/her somewhere, make sure his/her feet are securely on the foot rest. If there is no foot rest on the wheelchair, ask the nursing staff for them. If no footrests are available, ask the person to lift up his/her feet. Walk a little slower and watch their feet to make sure the person does not drop his/her feet while you are moving. If his/her feet drop, they might catch on the floor and get caught under the wheelchair risking a broken ankle. Lock the brakes when you reach your destination.

Do not offer food or drink to a resident in a nursing home if you don't know their dietary restrictions.

To avoid risking injury to yourself or the other person, never lift or physically assist an older adult from a bed or wheelchair.

Do not assist the person to the bathroom. Inform the staff and ask them to assist the person. Remember, you are a visitor, not a care provider.

If you are visiting someone in a care facility and you see an isolation sign on or beside the door, or a box on the door with isolation equipment, check with staff before entering the room. If you need to put on isolation equipment, follow these procedures:

Masks, gowns, and gloves are put on before entering the room.

There should be a red lined container in the person's room into which you dispose gowns, masks, and gloves when leaving the room. Take gown off first. Take gloves off second. Peel gloves off starting from the wrist turning gloves inside out as you take them off. After you have removed the first glove, slide your finger under the inside of the second glove and peel off from the inside out. Take mask off last by taking hold of the elastic band behind your ears.

When washing hands, use soap and warm water. Wash hands for at least 20 seconds making sure you scrub your fingernails, between your fingers, under rings, and up the wrist. When you are finished washing your hands, do not turn off the water. Dry your hands first, then turn the water off using a dry paper towel. Remember: you turned the water on with contaminated hands; turning the water off before drying your hands will re-contaminate them.

A temporary alternative to hand washing is the use of disinfectant hand gel which is usually available in dispensers on the walls in the hallways or in the person's room. Thoroughly rub the gel into your hands, especially in-between your fingers, until your hands are dry. The hand gel is only effective if you rub them thoroughly into the skin.

Visitation Tips

Be intentional about your visit. If you aren't, you may not be prepared for the emotional toll the visit may make on you. The best way to prepare yourself is to first have a quiet meditation, read Scripture, or pray. Be attentive to God's presence; ask for strength and guidance.

As an ambassador of Jesus Christ, you need to be intentionally aware of God's presence. Miller writes, "Each member of the ministry team should learn to become comfortable with the process of opening him/herself to God in the lifting up of the heart, in talking to God on the way to the visit, in being the partner alongside God as he/she enters the doorway, in meeting God in the room within, in letting God in him/her find God in the person visited and so be drawn together."[3]

You also need to be prepared to read Scripture and pray with the person you are visiting. Ask God to give you a Scripture, maybe one that has really spoken to you lately, or one that will specifically address the shut-in's unique needs. Before you leave, ask the person for permission to read a Scripture and pray for him/her. Don't assume he/she will want it. Jesus never forced himself on anyone, and you shouldn't either. Forcing him/her to accept Scripture reading and prayer without permission may spoil any chances for future ministry.

The length of each visit should be determined by the condition of the person whom you are visiting, the person's routine, and the presence of family or other visitors.

Visiting a nursing home resident is always unpredictable, even when visiting someone whom you have visited before, as there may have been a change in his/her condition. When visiting someone for the first time, you won't always know what to expect. The person may be hearing or vision impaired, unable to speak, hooked up to various machines, suffering from dementia, or may be experiencing other forms of declining health.

If a nursing home resident complains about the care he/she is receiving, ascertain if the complaint is legitimate. One of the best ways to do that is by asking specific questions as to when, where, how, and who. If the response is rather vague or the person has dementia, there may not be much validity to the complaint. However, you should also share these concerns with the nurse, especially if there appears to be some truth to what you have been told.

Sensitivity

The art of communication does not begin with having the "gift of gab." It begins with being sensitive to the needs of the person whom you are visiting. This involves accepting the person for who he/she is as a unique individual whom God has created in His image.

Sensitivity also means:

Allow the person to express his/her feelings without being judgmental or critical about the way he/she feels.

Take an interest in those things which are of interest to the person—family, hobbies, church, sports, cooking, etc. Photographs, knickknacks, or other things in the room may indicate the person's interests.

Keep at eye level and maintain eye contact.

Be aware of the person's need for rest and do not overstay your welcome.

Pay attention to the person—don't fidget, don't stare past the person, and don't be distracted by the surroundings.

Communicating

Communication is: 55% body language; 38% tone of voice; only 7% words.

Forms of communicating:
- Verbal: What you say, how you say it.
  - Non-verbal: Body language.

Negative forms of communicating:
- Verbal:
  - Talking down to the person—demeaning, baby talk.
  - Unsympathetic to his/her needs.
  - Interrupting his/her story.
  - Negative tone of voice.
- Non-verbal:
  - Not making eye contact.
  - Fidgeting.
  - Looking away.
  - Sloppy appearance.

Building mutual trust through communicating:
- Be honest.
- Be open.
- Accept others as they are.
- Respect others.
- Active listening.
- Hear/listen to the silence.

The best way to make eye contact is to come down to the person's level by pulling up a chair in front of him/her. Towering above the person if he/she is in a wheelchair or in a bed, makes it difficult for him/her to see and hear you.

If a person is hearing impaired, speaking louder may not necessarily help him/her to hear you. Lower the pitch of your voice and speak clearly and slowly. Don't use abbreviations such as aren't, isn't, wasn't, etc., because he/she may not hear the "n't." If his/her impairment is only in one ear, speak into the other. Ask permission to turn off the television or radio to eliminate background noise.

Ask non-threatening, open-ended questions. Yes/no questions do not lead into a conversation. However, for people with dementia, open-ended questions may be too confusing. Use your best judgment as to which types of questions you ask. Some examples of open-ended questions are:

- How was your day today?
- What do/did you do for a living?
- How is it different from your own home?
- What did you like to do as a child?
- I have four children and six grandchildren. Do you have any?
- What do/don't you like about living here?

Other conversation starters could include these questions:

- (Seeing knickknacks on a shelf) These knickknacks look like they came from another country. What country are they from? Did you visit that country? Was your visit to that country a vacation or was it work related?
- (Looking at photos on the wall) Is this your grandson in the army uniform? Is he still in the army? Where is he stationed? Did you also serve in the military?
- (Seeing books or magazines scattered around the room) I see you like to read. What kind of books/magazines do you like? Who is your favorite author?
- (Noticing a piano in the room) What kind of music do you like to play? How old were you when you first started playing? Did you teach music?
- Sharing similar experiences, vocations, or hobbies also helps to engage the person in a meaningful conversation.

For people who are unable to communicate verbally, someone who is of sound mind may respond to yes/no questions by squeezing your hand or by eye movements. Examples: one squeeze for yes, two for no; one eye blink for yes, two for no; upward glance of the eyes for yes, downward glance for no.

Another way to communicate with non-verbal residents is by using a letter board as per the following sample. You can easily make one yourself using a piece of cardboard.

A	B	C	D	E	F	G	H	I
J	K	L	M	N	O	P	Q	R
S	T	U	V	W	X	Y	Z	1
2	3	4	5	6	7	8	9	0

If the person is not vision impaired, hold the letter board so the he/she can see it. Point to the first row and ask, "Is it in this row?" If not, go down to the next row. When you get to the correct row, ask, "Is it (and then name each letter)? If the person is vision impaired, you may need to verbally recite the entire alphabet until you get to the correct letter. Both of these processes will require you to have pen and paper so that you can write down the response. This type of communication is slow and tedious requiring a lot of time and patience as the person spells out a sentence letter by letter. However, the person will be very appreciative of you for doing this.

Someone with dementia might use present tense verbs when talking about the past, or might talk about the past as if it is present day reality. Don't try to correct him/her or argue as this will only cause the person to become agitated. Go along with the story. For example, if the person says that his/her mother is waiting at the bus stop after school, ask about his/her school or ask how his/her mother is doing. Remember that the person is reliving his/her childhood which is present day reality for him/her. Keep the conversation in that reality.

If the person is in a comatose like state, such as sometimes occurs as a result of brain injury, Alzheimer's disease, or shortly before death, assume the resident is able to hear. Depending on your knowledge of the person and your comfort level, talk to him/her about subjects of interest, read Scripture or poetry, sing hymns, and pray. Don't speak negatively in his/her presence.

Active Listening

Jesus frequently said, *"He who has ears to hear, let him hear."* (Matthew 11:15, et al.) It was His way of saying, "Listen carefully to what I am saying." We need to do the same when we visit someone. Miller states, "The skill of active listening is a way to learn how to see and hear that involves understanding and caring. To be an active listener is to hear and see with the heart."[4]

To be an active listener involves fully engaging with the person, not letting your mind wander onto other things but keeping it focused on what the person is saying. It also involves observing the person's body language (voice, gestures, breathing, muscle tension, posture, clothing, appearance)—what is that saying?

- Active listening also includes:
- Paraphrasing and repeating back to the person what you think the person is telling you.
- Not being judgmental, critical, or argumentative.
- Not interrupting the person or finishing his/her sentences.

Following these simple guidelines will make your visit more enjoyable and meaningful for both you and the person you are visiting.

Bibliography

Preface

1 A Late Frost: Reflection on Aging, Minneapolis, MN: Sunmark Productions, 1993.

Chapter 1

1 Keith G. Meador and Shaun C. Henson. Growing Old in Christ. Edited by Stanley Hauerwas, Carole Bailey Stoneking, Ketih G. Meador and David Cloutier, (Grand Rapids: Wm. B. Eerdmans Publishing, 2003), p. 100

2 Carole Bailey Stoneking. Growing Old in Christ, p. 80

3 Stanley Hauerwas and Laura Yordy. Growing Old in Christ, p. 169

4 Carole Bailey Stoneking. Growing Old in Christ, p. 74

5 Richard B. Hays and Judith C. Hays. Growing Old in Christ, p. 11

Chapter 2

1 Joel James Shuman. Growing Old in Christ, p. 165

2 Susan Pendleton Jones and L. Gregory Jones. Growing Old in Christ, p. 196

Chapter 3

1 David Kessler. The Needs of the Dying: a guide to bringing hope, comfort, and love to life's final chapter (New York: HarperCollins Publishers, 2001) p. 5

2 Susan Pendleton Jones and L. Gregory Jones. Growing Old in Christ, p. 197

3 M. Therese Lysaught. Growing Old in Christ, p. 298

4 David Kessler. The Needs of the Dying. p. 160

Chapter 5

1 David Kessler. The Needs of the Dying. p. 152

Chapter 6

1 David Cloutier. Growing Old in Christ, p. 247

2 Joel James Shuman. Growing Old in Christ, p. 151

3 David Kessler. The Needs of the Dying. p. 2

4 Ibid.

5 Ibid, p. 8

Addendum

1 Kent C. Miller. Ministry to the Homebound: A 10-Session Training Course (San Jose: Resource Publications, Inc., 1995) p. 40

2 Ibid. p. 43

3 Ibid. p. 87

4 Ibid. p. 96

Johannes "John" Hoogerbrugge

John was born in the Netherlands in 1949, immigrated to Canada in 1952 and to the United States in 1974. He is a 1974 graduate of Elim Bible Institute and College and received his MDiv from Pittsburgh Theological Seminary in 2003.

John has served as pastor of two churches, worked for twenty years as a long-term health care chaplain, and ministered in several foreign countries.

This manuscript, God's Forgotten Pillars, was written from his experience as a long-term health care chaplain after ministering to thousands of elderly patients, many of whom were neglected by their own churches.

John lives in a small town just north of Pittsburgh, PA, with his wife Dawn. They have four children and eight grandchildren.

For more information, he can be contacted at:

gfpillars@gmail.com.